INTRODUCTION TO THUMB POSITION

(Cello)

T0057056

A. W. BENOY
and
L. SUTTON

MUSIC DEPARTMENT

OXFORD
UNIVERSITY PRESS

INTRODUCTION TO THUMB POSITION
(Cello)

by A. W. Benoy and L. Sutton

PART I

(No extensions or changes in the position of the thumb required)

Part II (for which extensions and changes in the position of the thumb are required) is on page 11

© 1965 Oxford University Press
Printed in Great Britain
OXFORD UNIVERSITY PRESS, MUSIC DEPARTMENT, GREAT CLARENDON STREET, OXFORD OX2 6DP
Photocopying this copyright material is ILLEGAL.

Irish Love Song

(Believe me, if all those endearing young charms)

Andante con moto

6.

p expressivo

p

poco rall.

a tempo

p

dim.

Exercise

Moderato

7.

mf

Gaelic Lullaby

Moderato

8.

p

cresc.

p

Scandinavian Dance

(Cochin China)

Allegro spiritoso

9.

f

To Wander

Old French Carol

(La Ballade de Jésus Christ)

Old French Carol

(Noël Nouvelet)

Shepherds' Song

(from Quintet, L' Uccelliera)

English Folk Song

(The Tailor and the Mouse)

Pavane

Peaceful Slumbering Ocean
Andante tranquillo
Storace
22.
mf
p
Hornpipe
Allegro giocoso
23.
f
The Dashing White Sergeant
Allegro vivo
24.
f
mf
cresc.
f
mf
cresc.
f

How blest are shepherds

(King Arthur)

Purcell

Staines Morris

Country Dance

Gavotte

Mozart

Polka
Allegro
29.
f
30.
31.
32.
33.
London New
Moderato
34.
f
con dignite
Ecossaise
Allegretto
Beethoven
35.
f
mf
f
mf
f

May Song

Waltz

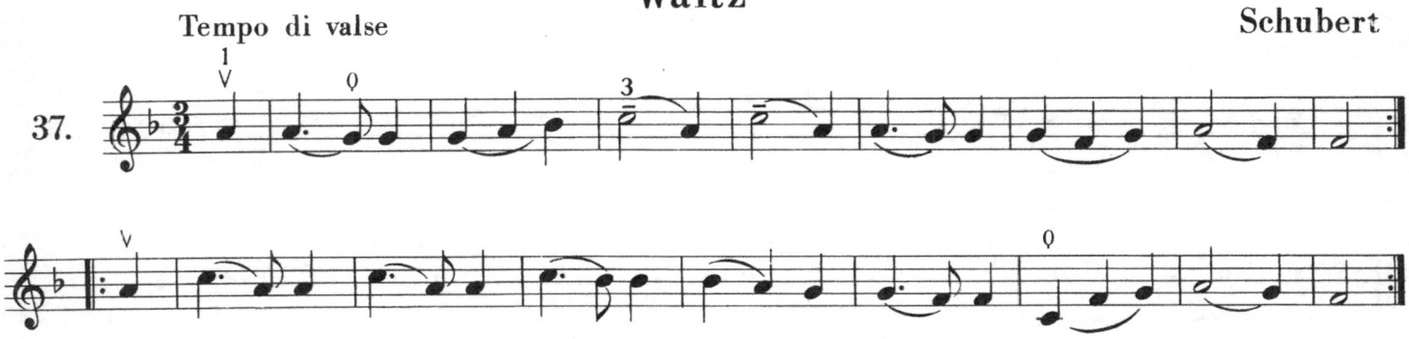

French Popular Song

Trumpet Tune

(King Arthur)

Purcell

Savez-vous planter les choux

Duke Street

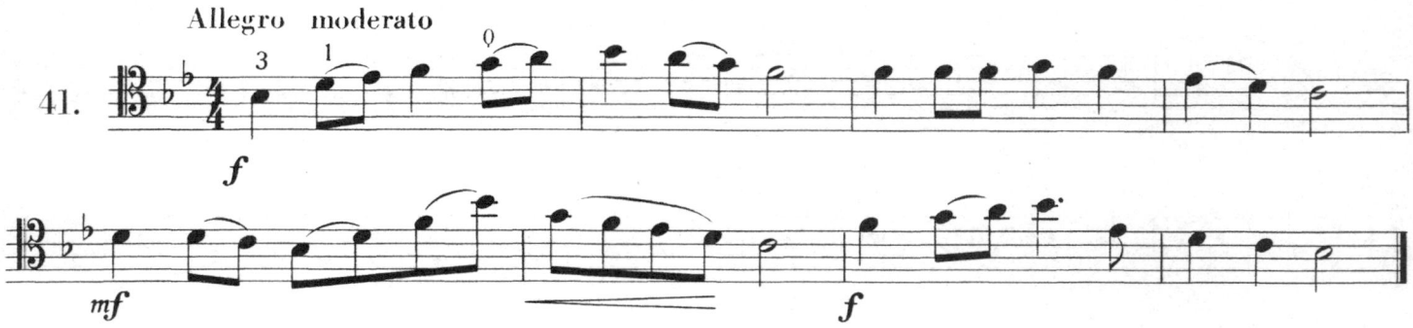

Bohemian Waltz

(Der Freischütz)

Weber

PART II

(Extensions and changes in the position of the thumb required)

Country Dance

(The Pirates' Waltz)

German Folk Song

(Be kind, gentle Shepherdess)

Contentment

German Folk Song

(Awake, my heart's desire)

Scottish Traditional Song

(A Rosebud by my early walk)

Country Dance

(The Phoenix)

Minuet
Moderato
Handel
54.
f
mf
f
p
cresc.
f

Country Dance
(The Devil among the Tailors)
Allegro
55.
mf
f
mf
cresc.
f

Country Dance
(The Marquis of Lorne)
Allegro
56.
f
mf
f

Cradle Song

Andante tranquillo

Schubert

57.

p

mp

p

He shall feed his flock

(Messiah)

Larghetto

Handel

58.

p

poco cresc.

p

Allegretto

(Octet in E)

Allegretto

Spohr

59.

p

mf

p

Reproduced and printed by
Halstan & Co. Ltd., Amersham, Bucks., England